D1743417

First published in the UK in 2011 by The Salariya Book Company Ltd
Originally created and designed by David Salariya

Revised edition published in the UK in 2025 by Hatch Press,
an imprint of Bonnier Books UK
4th Floor, Victoria House
Bloomsbury Square, London WC1B 4DA
Owned by Bonnier Books
Sveavägen 56, Stockholm, Sweden
www.bonnierbooks.co.uk

Copyright © 2025 by Hatch Press

1 3 5 7 9 10 8 6 4 2

All rights reserved

ISBN 978-1-83587-1454

Edited by Rebecca Kealy
Production by Nick Read

Printed in the UK

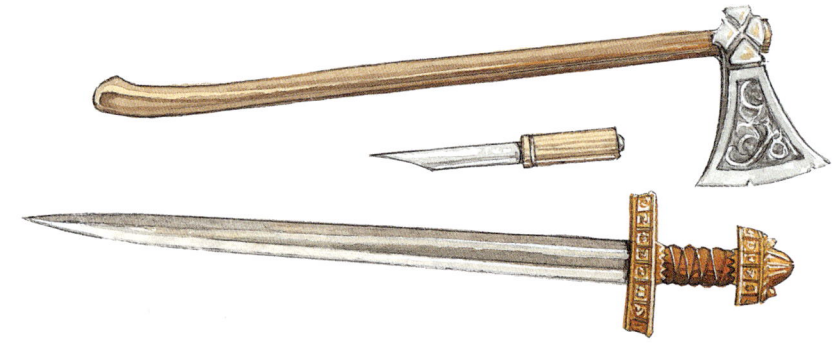

You Wouldn't Want to...

BE A
VIKING EXPLORER!

Written by Andrew Langley

Illustrated by David Antram

Hatch

Contents

Introduction

The Viking people originally lived in small communities in Scandinavia, northern Europe, raising crops and livestock, fishing, and trading goods with their neighbours. Each community was ruled by a king or 'chieftain'. By around 790 CE, the population had grown too large, so the Vikings began to explore other lands in search of territory and booty. Raiders crossed the sea to attack England, Ireland and Scotland. With their swift, long ships and bloodthirsty ways, they terrified coastal villages and seized large areas of land.

By the 850s, the Vikings of Sweden and Norway had established powerful trading towns in northern Europe. Norwegian settlers began to colonise Iceland, where the climate was much like their homeland's, and a century later, a Viking called Erik the Red reached Greenland and set up a new colony. In the tenth century, Leif Ericsson was the first Viking to cross the unknown ocean to the west and venture to North America.

As an adventurous young Viking, you are eager to join another group of explorers who plan to follow in Leif's footsteps in search of a new life. You will travel vast distances across the Atlantic Ocean to the coast of a new continent. It will be a difficult and dangerous journey – you really wouldn't want to be a Viking explorer!

5

Greenland: Time to Escape

Vikings first discovered Greenland in about 982. Their leader, Erik the Red, thought it was a fine place for a settlement, so he sailed back to Iceland and told his people. Erik called it 'green land' to make them think there was rich soil for farming as well as caribou and fish for food and bears and foxes to hunt for their furs. Hundreds of Vikings followed him to the new country, and you were one of them. But what a disappointment! The land is not very green at all – it is bitterly cold and few crops grow. How can you escape to find a better life?

The Viking World

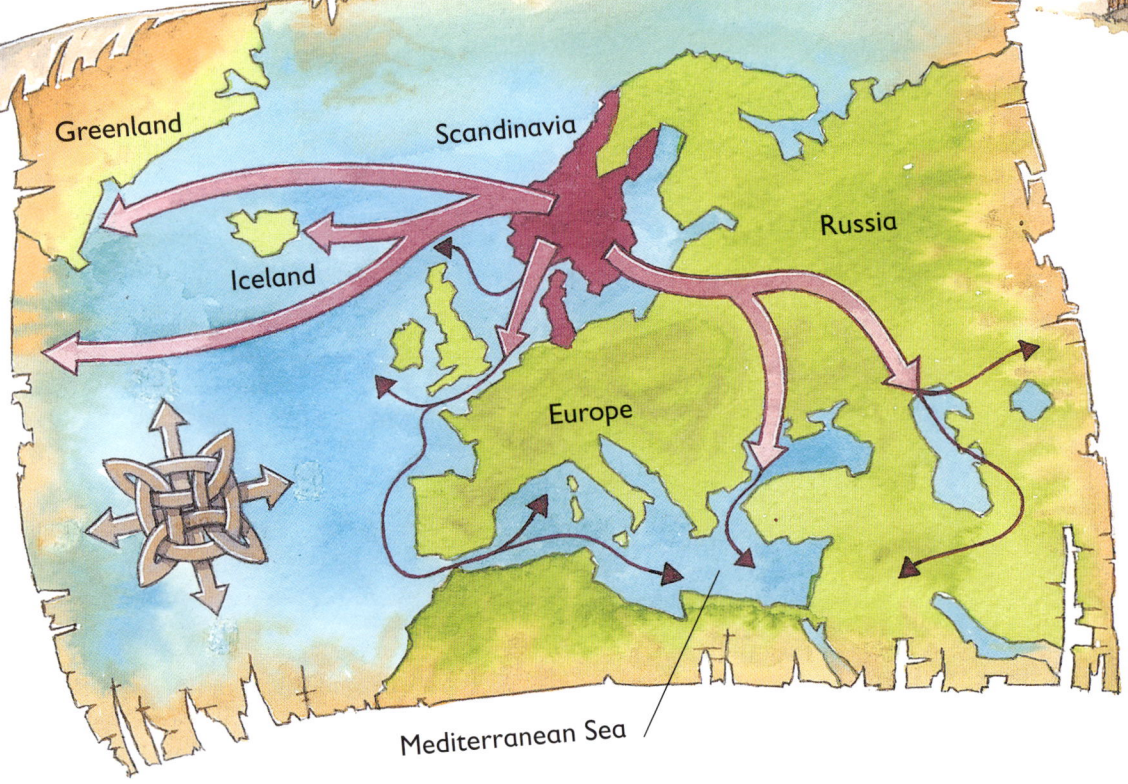

The Vikings spread out from Scandinavia in search of new land and freedom from their harsh rulers. Some went across Europe, reaching Russia and the Mediterranean. Others travelled west to what is now known as Iceland, Greenland and North America.

My name is Radnor Lothbrok (hairy trousers). My life is dull, dull, dull. . .

Handy hint

Nasty smell!

Try to avoid living near your town's workshop, where they make leather from animal skins. The stink is disgusting!

Choose me!

SAILORS WANTED
Thorvald, Leif Ericsson's brother, is planning an expedition! He is going to explore another new land across the sea to the west, and wants brave men to row his ship. You volunteer at once, eager for some adventure.

The Long Ship

Members of the crew load the ship with food, water and other supplies for the voyage. The ship is long and narrow, made from oak planks that curve upward at each end. The planks are fitted together with iron nails, and any gaps are plugged with tar and animal hair. The distance from the bottom to the gunwale is only around 1.8m, and along each side are 16 holes for the oars to slide through. These holes can be shut in rough weather to stop the water from coming in.

What Will You Take?

There is not much room aboard. Most of the cargo has to be stored in the narrow space under the deck. You are taking weapons and tools, as well as casks of water. The hens and goats travelling with you will supply fresh eggs and milk.

Shield

Clothes

Axe

Drinking horn

Sack of grain

Cooking pot

Handy hint

Handy hint

In rough seas, the boat will need bailing out with buckets. You don't want to sink!

Come on Bjorn! I don't know where we're going either!

OFF YOU GO
You sit down on your sea chest and grip your oar. The helmsman stands at the stern, and Thorvald, the chieftain, stands at the bow. He gives an order and all 32 of you pull on the oars. The adventure has begun!

Life at Sea

TAKING A BREAK
Once the sail is up, the wind drives the ship along. You can put away your oar and relax. There is no shelter on deck, but you soon get used to the cold.

EATING
In good weather, you can go ashore at night and light a fire for cooking. In bad weather, the ship stays at sea and you have to chew on cold, dried fish.

SLEEPING
To keep warm at night, you snuggle inside a skin sack called a 'hudfat', normally used for storing tools. But you have to share it with someone else!

Each member of the crew pulls hard on their oars. The long ship moves away from the shore, and a wind springs up. Thorvald orders you to stop rowing and raise the mast. It's made from a tall pine tree trunk, which the crew members place in a slot in the middle of the ship and haul upright. Together, they then hoist the heavy, cloth woollen sail. It fills with wind and the ship quickly gathers speed. The helmsman uses an oar attached to the stern, keeping the coast on the starboard (right-hand) side.

Come on, Short Erik! Push!

Short Erik

Handy hint

If you can't see land, watch the flight of seabirds. They will always fly in the direction of land!

Into the Unknown

Groan

SEASICKNESS
The swell of the sea makes you feel sick, headachy, and sleepy. But after a couple of days, you get used to the motion of the ship and feel better.

On the second day, the ship sails farther from land. Soon you are in the open sea and will depend on the skills of the helmsman and the chieftain to take you in the right direction. This is a difficult job, for rain is pelting down and the wind whips up the waves. The freezing rain has soaked through your leather clothing, and there is not a dry place to sit. Slabs of ice drift past the ship, showing that the Arctic ice pack is not far away to the north. The sail is lowered to prevent it from being split by the howling gales, and Thorvald orders everyone to get their oars ready. Rowing makes it easier for the helmsman to steer and avoid the dangerous ice floes.

STEERING BY THE STARS
By night, the helmsman finds his course by looking for the North Star, always exactly north in the night sky. By day, he steers by the position of the sun.

BRAVE EXPLORERS
From Scandinavia, Vikings sailed the unknown to reach the Faeroe Islands, Iceland and then to Greenland. In 992, Vikings became the first Europeans to land in what is now known as North America.

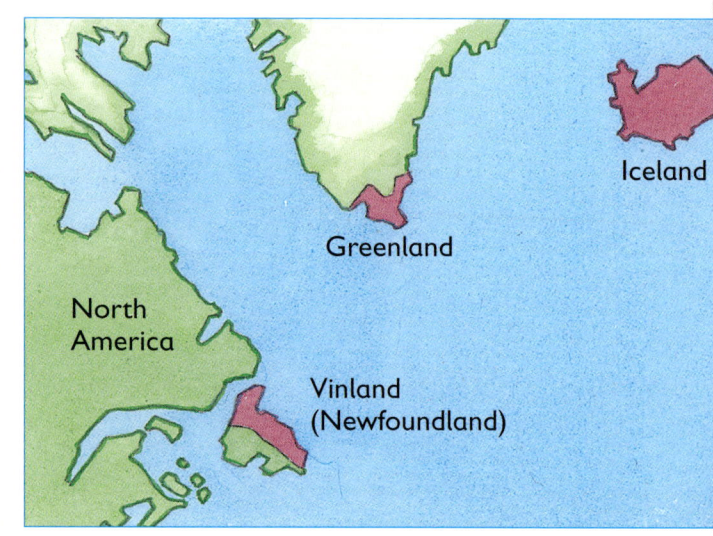

North America

Greenland

Iceland

Vinland (Newfoundland)

13

Lost! Drifting in a Fog

Once the wind has died down, a thick mist swirls around the ship and chills you to the bone in your soaking wet clothes. The only thing that keeps you warm is the effort of rowing. Worse still, you cannot see anything, and both the sun and the ice floes have disappeared behind the fog. Which course should the helmsman steer? You need to ask for help from the gods. The Viking religion is part of your daily life, with no special priests or temples. Thorvald is the chieftain, so he prays to Odin, the father of all the gods, and to Thor, the god of the sky and ruler of storms.

Finding the Way

It is easy to navigate when you can see the coast: you simply follow a series of known landmarks. In open sea, it is more difficult. Avoiding icebergs and pack ice can easily send you off course.

We're lost!

HERE COMES THE SUN

The gods answer the prayers, and the sun breaks through the clouds. The helmsman can now figure out the course westward – the direction taken by the two expeditions that have made the voyage before.

Steam

Steam

Handy hint

Slop

Every few days, rub the fat from sheep or other animals into your goatskin boots. This will keep them soft and waterproof.

We're not lost. We just don't know where we are.

FINDING LAND
Thorvald followed the route taken by his brother Leif, heading west across the sea until he saw land.

BEACHING THE BOAT
The crew must leap ashore and grab ropes to haul the ship as far up the beach as they can. This will stop it from being washed away.

LEIF ERICSSON
Son of Erik the Red, sailed west in around the year 1000 in search of new land and timber supplies.

The next morning, you are awoken by a crew member. "Land ahead!" he shouts. You can see from the ship that the coast of this new land is mountainous and icy, with no grass or trees. Thorvald recognises this as Helluland, or 'flat rock land', the place Leif Ericsson had described after his own voyage. The helmsman turns the ship to follow the coast southward, and the landscape becomes more promising. . .

Leif landed on the coast of North America (probably Newfoundland).

You reach what Leif called Markland, or 'wood land', which is flat and thickly covered with forests. Finally, you arrive at Vinland, or 'wine land', where the climate is warmer. Thorvald leads his crew ashore. But what dangers are lurking?

Handy hint

Use tree trunks as rollers to haul your ship over land. This means you can bypass any waterfalls and rapids that would stop your progress up a river.

Grrrr

Making Wine

The first job is to build a large hut. Tools and equipment are brought ashore, and a site is found that is flat and sheltered from the wind. Some men cut down trees, shape the timbers and make the building's framework. You stay and dig up sods of turf to cover the roof and walls. These walls are over a metre thick and will keep everyone warm in winter when a fire is burning in the stone hearth.

GATHERING THE BERRIES
Huge red huckleberries grow here. You can turn them into wine!

CRUSHING
Put the berries in to a bucket and squash them with a piece of wood. Then leave the juice to ferment into wine.

Squash

Squash

DRINKING
Making wine is a good way to preserve the juice of wild fruits. You can drink the wine through the cold winter.

Pity we ate Bjorn – he'd have enjoyed this grass.

18

Handy hint

Hundreds of seabirds have nests on the coast's cliffs. Steal their eggs to make a quick meal.

FISHING

The sea is full of fish such as cod and herring, and there are salmon and eels in the rivers. All these can be dried and salted to preserve them for winter.

Winter in Vinland

In Greenland, the winters are long and extremely cold, with short days and many hours of darkness. But Vinland is a lot farther south, so summer here is much longer and winter not so cold. There is less snow, and grass continues to grow for most of the year. All the same, you have to spend many winter evenings huddled around the smoky fire in your hut. You pass the time by telling each other tales about the great deeds of ancient heroes and gods, such as the terrifying Thor and his mighty hammer, Mjollnir.

EXPLORING INLAND

In summer, Thorvald leads an expedition into the mountains and forests to the west. You find the lakes full of fish and the woods full of animals such as bears, deer and antelopes.

Thor

Valkyrie

CARVING

Many Vikings are skilled at carving objects from wood or bone. They make figures of gods, or everyday items like spoons and bowls.

Frey

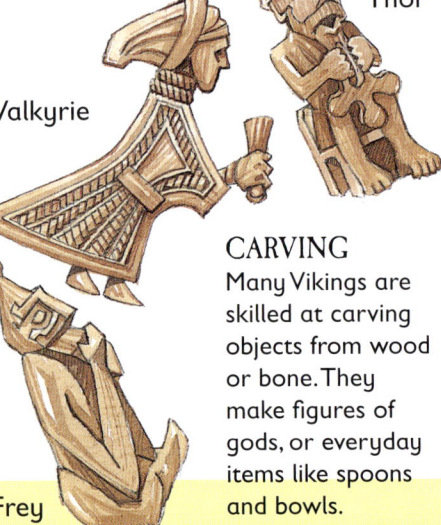

BOARD GAMES

You all like to play hnefatafl (pronounced 'nefatal'), a game like chess, where you move pieces to try and capture the king.

21

Skraelings!

The First Americans

Thousands of years ago, an ice cap joined the continents of Asia and North America.

The first American peoples probably walked over the ice from Asia into North America about 20,000 years ago. From here, they slowly spread out and made settlements. The Vikings called them 'skraelings'.

The skraelings were hiding under their boats, made of seal or moose skins stretched over wooden frames.

One day, you find three rocks on the seashore, but they seem to be made of wood or leather. You and your companions tip them over, and there, huddled underneath, are some people! You had no idea anybody else lived in this remote place. The strangers jump up in panic, terrified at the sight of your weapons.

And don't pretend to be rocks again!

The Vikings are hostile to anyone who is not one of them and kill some of the strangers. Those who escape go back to their people, so the skraelings, or 'screaming barbarians', could now be planning a revenge attack. These skraelings were probably hunters who traveled south in search of seals and seabirds.

Handy hint

Always keep your sword sharp – you never know when you might need it!

Aaaagh!

Aaaagh!

23

Hunting and Storing Food

During autumn, you must gather and store enough food to last through the winter. There is wild wheat growing on the seashore, nuts and berries in the forest and plenty of animals to hunt for meat. The largest and most valuable prey are whales, which give a huge supply of meat as well as oil, skin and bones. But whale hunts are perilous. You must row out in a small boat and get as close to the whale as you can. One man hurls a harpoon. It sticks into the whale, which then starts to swim fast, dragging you along behind! Only when the whale becomes tired can you successfully catch it with spears.

Weapons

Axe

Dagger

Sword

Splash

Splash

BLACKSMITH AT WORK
Skilled Viking blacksmiths make anything, from axe-heads to cooking pots. Using tongs to hold hot metal on the anvil, they cut and hammer it into shape.

STORING FOOD
Fish and meat are preserved by hanging them to dry in the wind, or by 'pickling' in salty water. Even pine bark is stored to eat in case everything else runs out!

Helmet   Shield   Bow and arrows

Spear

Vikings are always
ready for a fight and
carry their weapons
with them at all times! They
protect their bodies with wooden
shields and iron helmets. They fight
with long-handled axes, double-edged
swords, iron-tipped arrows and spears for
throwing and jabbing. When they run into
battle, they sometimes howl like wolves to
terrify the enemy.

Handy hint

Deep freeze your meat by packing it in
ice and snow. This will stop it from rotting.

Whoosh!

Help! It's never
going to stop!

Under Attack!

You and Your Enemy

By the end of winter, you are all weak and very hungry. The food stores have been used up, and many of your companions have gotten sick. Everyone is feeling homesick for Greenland. You even hope to meet another band of skraelings to trade tools or cloth with in exchange for food.

Axes and swords with iron blades

HUNTER-GATHERERS
The skraelings are not as skilled as the Vikings when it comes to fighting. They aren't so obsessed with conquering land so spend most of their time hunting and gathering food instead.

GOING BERSERK
Viking warriors sometimes put on a 'ber-serk', or bearskin shirt, before going into battle, to help them fight ferociously. This is where we get the phrase 'going berserk'.

Flint-tipped arrows and spears

But when the skraelings return, they are not here to trade. They want revenge against those who attacked and killed their friends! They rush at you, shooting arrows and throwing spears. The iron weapons of the Vikings drive them off, but someone is hurt. Your chieftain lies fatally wounded by an arrow.

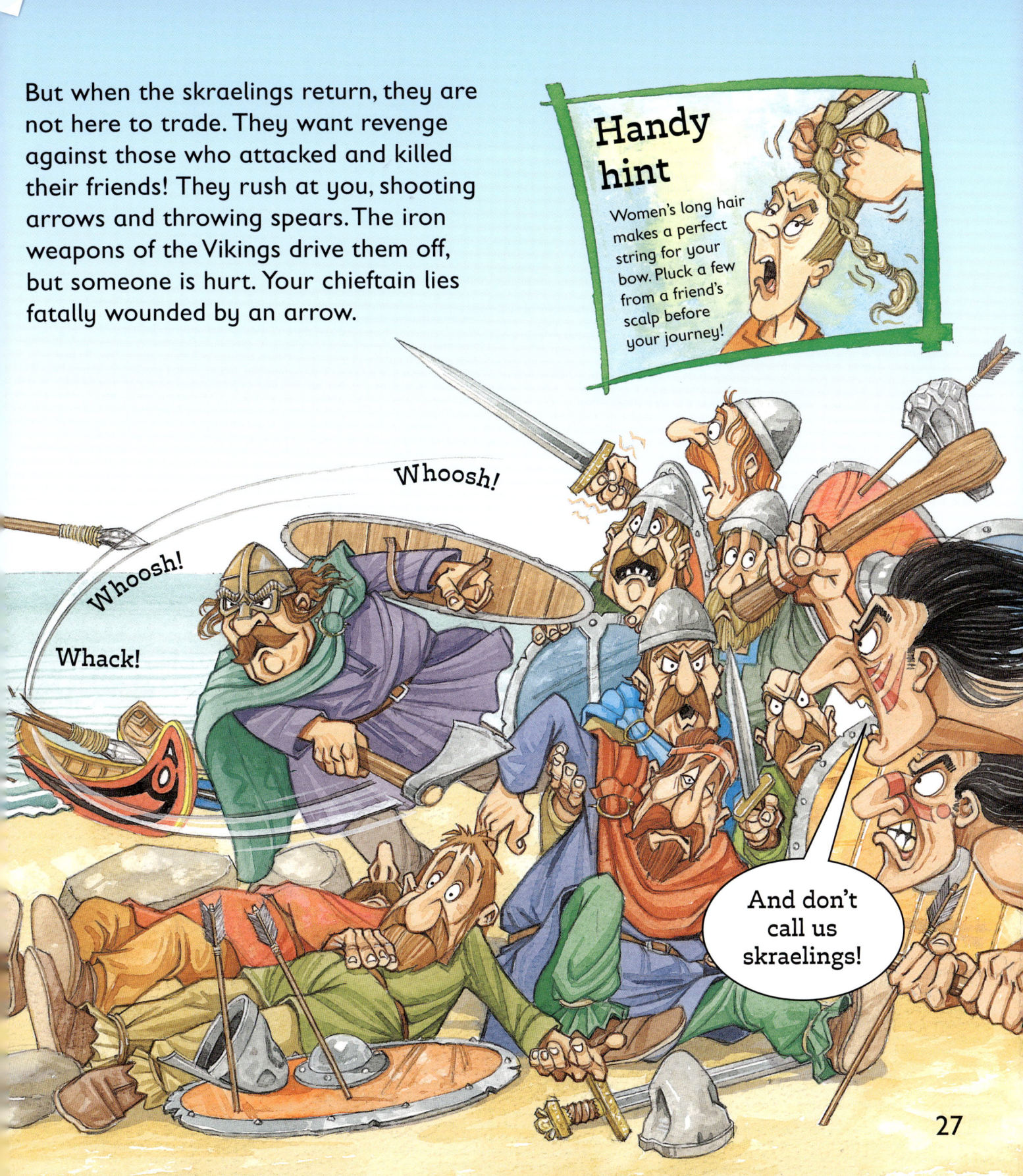

Handy hint

Women's long hair makes a perfect string for your bow. Pluck a few from a friend's scalp before your journey!

Whoosh!

Whoosh!

Whack!

And don't call us skraelings!

Going Home

Things are looking very bleak. The skraelings have retreated for the moment, but they'll be back. Chieftain Thorvald is dead, and many of your companions are wounded or ill. There is very little food available. The explorers have no choice but to sail back to Greenland. You load up the ship with tools and weapons and roll it down to the water's edge, ready for a quick getaway.

Harald

Alas, poor Thorvald. I knew him well, Harald.

LONG SHIP FUNERAL

Back at home, Thorvald's funeral would have been much grander. A Viking chief might be buried, or occasionally burned, inside a long ship that would carry him to the next world. With him went all he needed in the next life, including weapons, treasure, clothing and even horses.

FUNERAL PYRE

This is only a simple funeral. Animal hides are placed on the pyre with the body on top. The person's belongings, such as his weapons and drinking horn, are placed beside him.

Before you leave, there is a solemn task to perform. You pile up firewood on the beach and put Thorvald's body on top, surrounded by his belongings. Then you set fire to the funeral pyre. As you row away and begin the cold and dangerous journey home, you watch the flames roaring up into the sky.

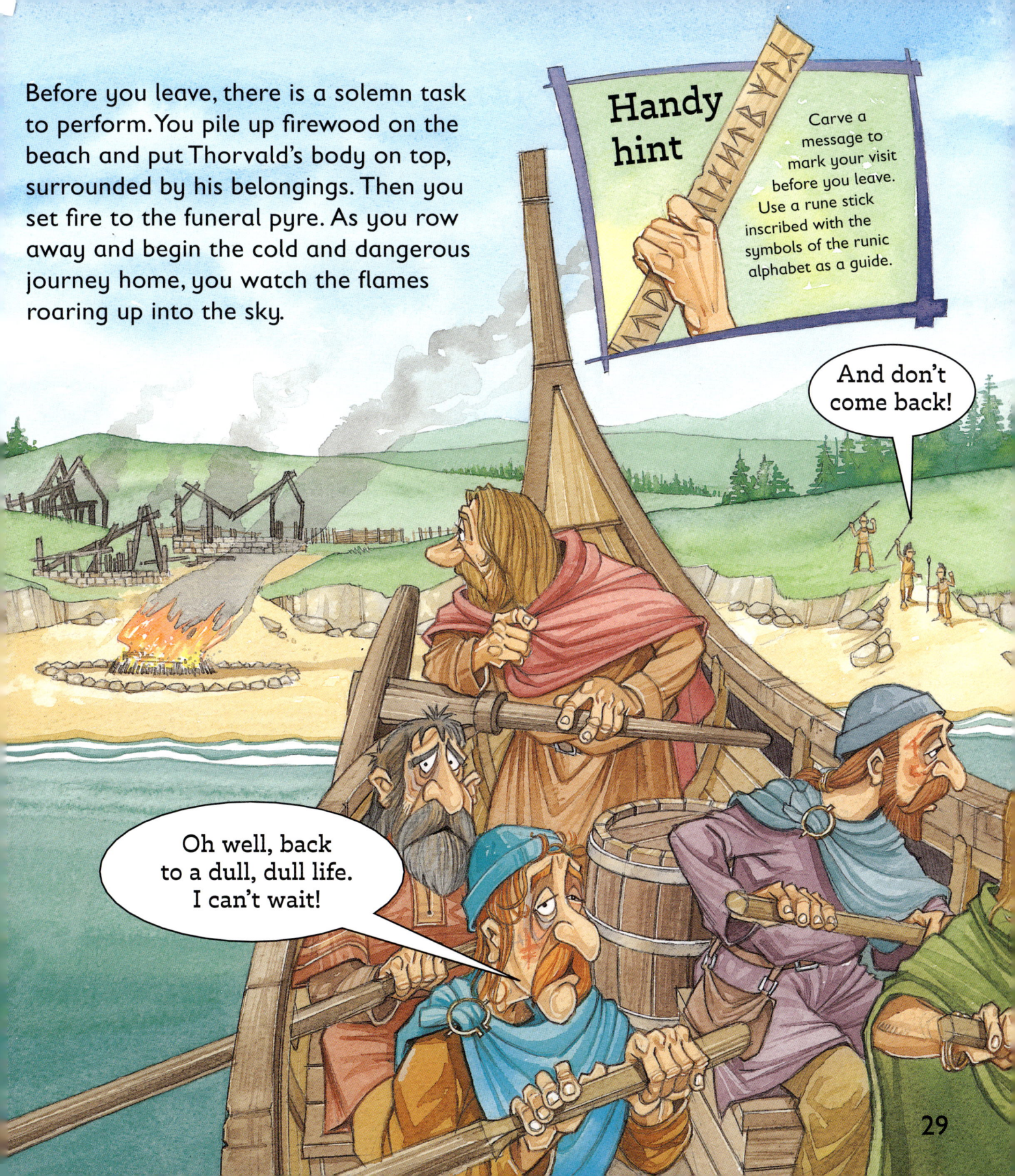

Handy hint

Carve a message to mark your visit before you leave. Use a rune stick inscribed with the symbols of the runic alphabet as a guide.

And don't come back!

Oh well, back to a dull, dull life. I can't wait!

Glossary

Antarctic The region in the far south of Earth, surrounding the South Pole.

Arctic The region in the far north of Earth, surrounding the North Pole.

Blizzard A storm with high winds blowing powdery snow.

Blubber The layer of fat found under the skin of seals and penguins. It keeps the animals warm and can be burned to provide light and heat.

Cairn A pile of stones or ice blocks, often built to mark paths or the summits of mountains.

Crevasse A deep crack in a glacier, sometimes hidden by snow.

Endurance The ability to withstand difficulties and stress for a long time. Also the name of Shackleton's ship.

Frostbite A condition caused by extreme cold, which destroys the tissues of the body. The ears, nose, toes and fingers are the areas most often affected by frostbite.

Glacier A river or large mass of ice, formed by packed-down snow. It flows very slowly from high ground down towards the sea.

Hazardous Extremely dangerous.

Hull The body of a ship.

Husky A powerful breed of dog used in the Arctic and Antarctic for pulling sledges.

Limpet A type of mollusc, with a shell and a muscular foot, that clings to rocks in the sea.

Sextant An instrument used by sailors to calculate their position at sea. It works by taking measurements of the position of the Sun and stars.

Stowaway A person who hides on board a ship so that he can travel for free.

Uncharted Not shown on any map.

Whaler A whale hunter or whaling ship.

Omen A happening or object believed to signal good or evil in the future.

Pack ice Large pieces of floating ice wedged together.

Rations A person's individual allowance of food and other supplies when there are shortages.

Rigging The ropes and wires attached to a ship's masts and sails.

Scurvy A disease, once common among sailors and polar explorers, caused by a lack of vitamin C.

Index